WHEN pets ATTACK!

CHIMPS AND MONKEYS ARE NOT PETS!

Gareth Stevens
Publishing

BY HEATHER MOORE NIVER

Please visit our website, www.garethstevens.com. For a free color catalog of all our high-quality books, call toll free 1-800-542-2595 or fax 1-877-542-2596.

Library of Congress Cataloging-in-Publication Data

Niver, Heather Moore.
Chimps and monkeys are not pets / by Heather Moore Niver.
    p. cm. — (When pets attack)
Includes index.
ISBN 978-1-4339-9289-6 (pbk.)
ISBN 978-1-4339-9290-2 (6-pack)
ISBN 978-1-4339-9288-9 (library binding)
1. Chimpanzees as pets — Juvenile literature. 2. Monkeys as pets — Juvenile literature. 3. Wild animals as pets—Juvenile literature. I. Niver, Heather Moore. II. Title.
SF459.C47 N58 2014
636.9885—dc23

First Edition

Published in 2014 by
Gareth Stevens Publishing
111 East 14th Street, Suite 349
New York, NY 10003

Copyright © 2014 Gareth Stevens Publishing

Designer: Katelyn E. Reynolds
Editor: Therese Shea

Photo credits: Cover, pp. 1, 19 Hemera/Thinkstock.com; cover, pp. 1–32 (home sweet home image) © iStockphoto.com/DNY59; cover, pp. 1–32 (background) Hemera/Thinkstock.com; cover, pp. 1–32 (blood splatter), pp. 3–32 (frame) iStockphoto/Thinkstock.com; p. 5 Attila Kisbenedek/AFP/Getty Images; pp. 7 (top), 13, 15, 21, 25, 29 iStockphoto/Thinkstock.com; p. 7 (bottom) Jupiterimages/Photos.com/ Thinkstock.com; p. 9 Thomas Marent/Visuals Unlimited, Inc./Getty Images; p. 11 Toni Angermayer/Photo Researchers/Getty Images; p. 12 Sharon Morris/Shutterstock.com; p. 17 Martin Harvey/Gallo Images/ Getty Images; p. 23 Dr. Clive Bromhall/Oxford Scientific/Getty Images; p. 27 John Foxx/Stockbyte/ Thinkstock.com; p. 28 Spencer Platt/Getty Images.

Printed in the United States of America

CPSIA compliance information: Batch #CS13GS: For further information contact Gareth Stevens, New York, New York at 1-800-542-2595.

CONTENTS

Words in the glossary appear in **bold** type the first time they are used in the text.

CRAZY CHIMPS AND MAD MONKEYS

There's no doubt about it: monkeys and chimpanzees are some of the coolest critters around. We love to see them at zoos and in the movies and read about them in books. Maybe monkeys and chimpanzees, or chimps, are so interesting because they're so much like us.

Having a monkey or a chimp as a pet might seem like it would be supercool. They're smart and fun. They can even learn how to use tools and computers. But chimps and monkeys are still wild animals. They're loud, messy, and even dangerous. Read on to learn why they should stay in the wild.

Jane GOODALL

In 1960, Jane Goodall was one of the first female scientists to travel into the wilderness of east Africa to study chimps. With careful and patient study, she made amazing discoveries. Jane learned that chimpanzees made their own tools. Before that, only humans were thought to make tools.

Jane Goodall is shown here with a chimp named Pola.

PART OF THE PRIMATE FAMILY

Monkeys and chimpanzees are both **primates**. Primates are **mammals**. Primates have hands and feet that can grip things. Their eyes are on the front of their head, facing forward, and they have large brains. Other primates include lemurs, orangutans, tarsiers, gorillas, and humans.

Most monkeys have tails, and apes don't. Chimpanzees are apes. Apes are closely related to humans. Chimps are some of the closest human relatives of all.

Monkeys and chimps are so similar to humans they seem like they'd be easy to care for—but they're not. Even in **captivity**, they're wild.

pretty much A PRIMATE

Primates such as monkeys and chimps are similar to other mammals, but certain features set them apart. Their feet have five fingers and flat nails instead of claws. They have a short muzzle, or jaw and nose. Primates have excellent eyesight, but they don't have a good sense of smell.

Monkeys that live in trees have longer tails than monkeys that spend a lot of time on the ground.

monkeys

chimpanzees

MONKEYS OLD AND NEW

There are more than 264 different species, or kinds, of monkeys. They are many shapes, sizes, and colors. Scientists group them based on where they live. The two basic groups of monkeys are Old World and New World. Baboons and other larger monkeys are Old World monkeys. They're found in Africa, central to southern Asia, Japan, and India. They live in rainforests and on **steppes**, islands, mountains, and **savannas**.

New World monkeys are smaller. They live in Mexico, Central America, and South America. They like **tropical** rainforests. Many New World monkeys have a prehensile tail. This means their tail can grab branches.

it's true! MONKEYS THROW THEIR POOP!

Monkeys and chimps may not be good pets for this reason alone: They throw their waste. When they feel threatened, scared, or bored, monkeys throw it at whatever bothers them. Yuck! Scientists think this is a sign of brain growth, though. Throwing waste as a message may be one step away from learning language.

Old World Monkeys, New World Monkeys

BODY PART	OLD WORLD	NEW WORLD
NOSE	small, curved **nostrils** set close together	round nostrils set far apart
CHEEK POUCHES	some have cheek pouches to store food	no cheek pouches
RUMP PADS	some have sitting pads on their rear end	no rump pad
TAIL	no prehensile tail	most have prehensile tail

A prehensile tail helps monkeys grab objects as tiny as peanuts.

GETTING AROUND

Some monkeys are terrestrial, which means they spend most of their time on the ground. Arboreal monkeys live up in the trees. Some arboreal monkeys use their prehensile tail to hang or keep them from falling.

Monkeys are well known for their in-air tricks. They're master jumpers. Colobus monkeys have extra long back legs, so they jump very far very quickly. Monkey feet are just as **flexible** as their hands, which is great for grabbing tiny treetop branches. Some monkeys have webbed toes that help them swim. They usually swim to get food or to avoid becoming food for a predator.

thumbs AND TOES

Old World monkeys and chimpanzees have opposable thumbs and toes. This means the thumb and toe can touch the other fingers and toes and grasp things. People have opposable thumbs, and it's a good thing we do. Try eating without using your thumb. It's not easy!

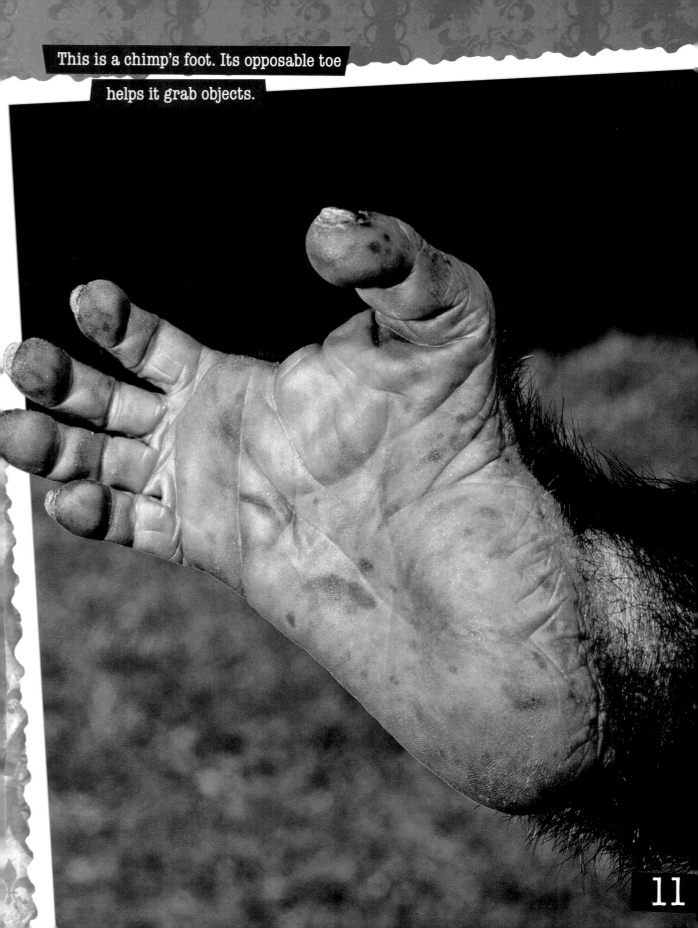

This is a chimp's foot. Its opposable toe helps it grab objects.

Gorillas and orangutans knuckle-walk, just like this chimp.

bonobo: NO CHIMP

Chimpanzees spend most of their day swinging from branch to branch in the trees, which is called brachiating (BRAY-kee-ay-ting). Their arms are longer than their legs, which is perfect for this style of travel.

Scientists once thought bonobos were just smaller chimps, so they called them "pygmy chimpanzees." Then, they realized bonobos were different. They're much less **aggressive** than chimps. Bonobos are comfortable walking upright, too. Bonobos are rare, but they're one of the smartest animals in the world.

Chimps also get around on all fours. They make fists and walk on their knuckles like feet. This is called knuckle walking. Chimps can walk on two legs, too, but they only do so when they need to carry something in their hands.

Most people don't have enough space for a pet chimp or monkey to walk around or enough trees for swinging.

This primate is a chimp-bonobo mix.

LOUD MOUTHS

Monkeys and chimps like to be heard. Chimps drum and bang on tree trunks. They make food calls to other chimps, a mix of grunts and barks. Chimps are so loud that chimps as far as 2 miles (3 km) away can hear them! Every chimp has its own "pant-hoot" sound, different from any other chimp's.

Monkeys also make loud sounds to say, "Keep out! This is my territory!" They use their voices so they don't have to fight. Monkeys bark, scream, grunt, hoot, moan, and wail to get their point across.

rain, rain GO AWAY

Think you don't like it when it rains? Howler monkeys live up to their name whenever it begins to rain or if they sense a rainstorm on the way. They howl together. Howler monkeys also howl first thing in the morning and at the end of the day.

Monkeys and chimps can be very loud. If they were your pets, you and your neighbors for miles around might not appreciate the noise!

TROOPS

A group of monkeys or chimps is called a troop. Troops move around together as they search for food. Chimps live in troops of up to 60. A monkey troop may be made up of a few monkeys or more than a thousand! Within a large troop, monkeys form smaller groups called harems. Harems have an adult male, a few adult females, and their children.

Every day, the monkeys and chimps in a troop **groom** each other. It's how the members of a troop bond. A grooming session can last just a few seconds or for hours.

less CROWDED

Not every kind of monkey likes to live in large groups. A few adult males without **mates** may hang around together. Gray titi monkeys live in small family units of two adults who are mates for life and their children. Titi monkeys live in Bolivia's tropical forests.

This baboon troop lives in a hilly region of Ethiopia.

RAISING BABIES

Baby monkeys, chimps, and other primates are cute and are often pulled away from their mothers to be sold as pets. Sadly, they miss out on learning about life in the wild. For example, bonobo babies can hardly do anything when they're first born. Their mothers need to carry them around for almost 2 years. Mothers protect and feed their babies. They also teach their children about hunting, grooming, and staying safe.

Both monkeys and chimps change as they grow up. They may become aggressive. They bite and scratch, which is natural for them in the wild but dangerous in a home.

unneeded GROWING PAINS

Sadly, when pet baby primates grow up, some owners try to control them by removing their teeth or fingernails. Many are chained or kept in a small space. The owner may finally give the primate to a special animal organization for care. By this time, it's too late for them to go back into the wild.

Mother monkeys make sure their babies get the kind of food they need to grow up healthy.

LARGE AND IN CHARGE

Monkeys and chimps can grow up to be big and heavy. The largest and heaviest monkey is the mandrill. It may be 30 inches (76 cm) tall and weigh 120 pounds (54 kg). An eastern African chimp can be 48 inches (1.2 m) tall and weigh 115 pounds (52 kg).

No matter how big or small, male chimps and monkeys try to prove their **dominance** in their group. Chimps, especially, want to be the troop leader. They try to scare away other males by slapping their hands, stamping their feet, dragging branches and sticks, and throwing rocks.

primate MEDICINE

Primates naturally want to prove they're in charge, which is another reason they're not good pets. Bites from primates can cause deep cuts and nasty **infections**. They may carry disease, too. And if your monkey or chimp is sick, few veterinarians are trained to treat it.

Mandrills are shy and live only in the tropical rainforests of Africa.

DON'T SMILE!

Primates communicate with touch and voice to avoid fighting, but they do fight. A toothy grin isn't a sign of friendliness to a chimp or monkey. When they see the teeth of another animal, they may think it's a sign of aggression or anger. Showing your teeth makes it look like you're about to bite! And monkeys and chimps may attack when they're scared or threatened.

Other actions of aggression include head bobbing and staring. Even scientists who work daily with monkeys and chimps say they can't let their guard down. They never know when they might be attacked.

Travis

A woman in Connecticut raised a chimp named Travis. Travis became famous around town and grew to weigh 200 pounds (91 kg). When he was 14 years old, Travis attacked his owner's friend, a woman he'd known for many years. Travis next attacked the police, who shot and killed him.

Chimps have four long, sharp teeth.

23

LOOKIN' GOOD

You've already read that grooming is an important way for primates to bond and communicate. Grooming helps these animals relax and keeps the group together. It's how they hang out! But just as importantly, grooming keeps their hair and skin healthy.

When grooming, monkeys and chimps use their fingers and teeth to comb through one another's hair. They remove dirt, insects, dead skin, and **parasites**. They may eat the bugs they find! Since chimpanzees and monkeys sometimes spend hours each day grooming, they'd miss out on this healthy bonding activity if kept as pets.

clean CHOMPERS

One monkey in Japan wants to keep her teeth in great shape. A Japanese macaque (muh-KAK) named Chonpe learned how to floss her teeth! She uses strands of her own hair to rub between her teeth. Chimpanzees, bonobos, and orangutans have been known to use sticks to keep their chompers healthy.

Grooming isn't just a two-primate activity. Often a whole group participates.

PRESERVE THE PRIMATES!

In 1900, more than 2 million chimpanzees lived across 25 countries. Now, only 150,000 to 300,000 chimps can be found in just a few African countries. They live in the Democratic Republic of Congo, Gabon, Central African Republic, Republic of Congo, and possibly Cameroon. Chimps are hunted for their meat, called bushmeat, or to sell to labs for testing. Chimps could become **extinct** within 15 years!

Monkeys aren't doing much better. They're the primates most often captured and sold as pets. They're also hunted for bushmeat. More than 40 percent of the 234 primate species are threatened with extinction.

save the FORESTS!

It's easy to lend a hand to save forest species in danger. First, don't buy anything made from their fur or body parts. You can also make sure any wood or paper items you purchase come from protected forests. For example, an FSC label means the products have come from companies that support **conservation**.

Monkeys and chimps become very stressed when caged. That's why zoos try to create surroundings similar to their homes.

These people are looking at a lowland gorilla in the Bronx Zoo's Congo Gorilla Forest exhibit.

Chimpanzees can live as long as 60 years. Some monkeys live to be 50 years old. Even if you did have the necessary space, tools, and skills to take care of a chimp or monkey, that's an awfully long time to be responsible for it. The kindest and safest way to care for chimps and monkeys is to learn about them but keep them in the wild.

You can learn about both chimps and monkeys in person at zoos. For example, New York City's Bronx Zoo has the Congo Gorilla Forest exhibit where visitors can visit all kinds of apes, monkeys, and other animals.

Some zoos do more than give us a chance to see rare animals up close. The Bronx Zoo gives part of the price of a ticket to efforts to save animals in danger of becoming extinct. The Lincoln Park Zoo in Chicago, Illinois, has a special program that teaches all about chimps and the threats they face.

older chimp

GLOSSARY

aggressive: acting with forceful energy while trying to cause harm

captivity: the state of being caged

conservation: the care of the natural world

dominance: the state of being the most powerful or strongest

extinct: no longer living

flexible: able to bend easily

groom: to clean fur, skin, or feathers

infection: the spread of germs inside the body, causing illness

mammal: a warm-blooded animal that has a backbone and hair, breathes air, and feeds milk to its young

mate: one of two animals that come together to make a baby

nostril: an opening through which an animal breathes

parasite: a living thing that lives in, on, or with another living thing, usually causing harm

primate: any animal from the group that includes humans, apes, and monkeys

savanna: a warm grassland with scattered patches of trees

steppe: a dry grassland with cold winters

tropical: having to do with the warm parts of Earth near the equator

FOR MORE INFORMATION

Books

De la Bédoyère, Camilla. *Monkeys & Apes*. Broomall, PA: Mason Crest Publishers, 2009.

Ellis, Carol. *Apes*. New York, NY: Marshall Cavendish Benchmark, 2011.

Moore, Heidi. *Chimpanzees*. Chicago, IL: Heinemann Library, 2012.

Websites

Center for Great Apes
www.centerforgreatapes.org
Check out news, view photos, and learn about rescued apes.

Howler Monkeys
kids.nationalgeographic.com/kids/animals/creaturefeature/howler-monkey/
Hear and learn about the loudest monkey of all.

The Jane Goodall Institute: Chimpanzees
www.janegoodall.org/chimpanzees
Read about chimpanzees, Goodall's studies, and how to save the chimps.

INDEX